MUSIC FROM
MINECRAFT

ISBN 978-1-7051-4217-2

HAL•LEONARD®

Visit Hal Leonard Online at
www.halleonard.com

Contact us:
Hal Leonard
7777 West Bluemound Road
Milwaukee, WI 53213
Email: info@halleonard.com

In Europe, contact:
Hal Leonard Europe Limited
42 Wigmore Street
Marylebone, London, W1U 2RN
Email: info@halleonardeurope.com

In Australia, contact:
Hal Leonard Australia Pty. Ltd.
4 Lentara Court
Cheltenham, Victoria, 3192 Australia
Email: info@halleonard.com.au

ALPHA
from MINECRAFT: VOLUME BETA

By DANIEL ROSENFELD

Moderately (♩ = ca. 100)

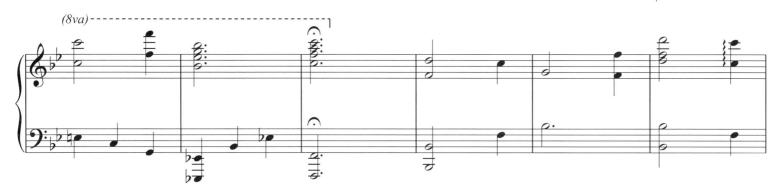

Slower (♩ = 90)

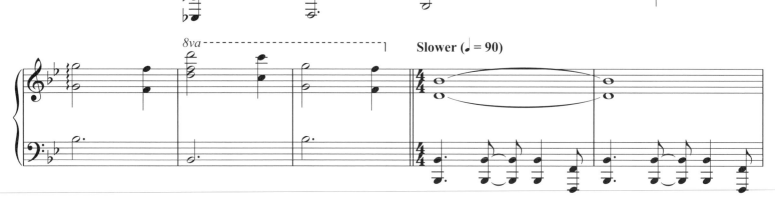

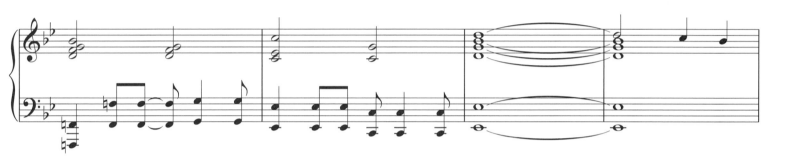

Faster (♩ = 123)

8vb -

8vb -

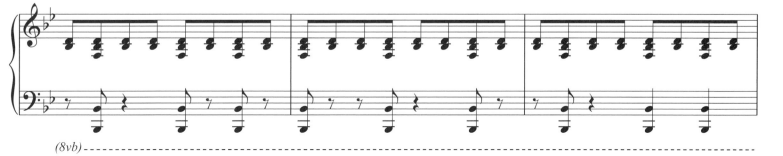

(8vb) -

6

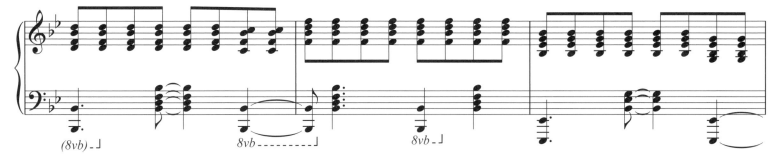

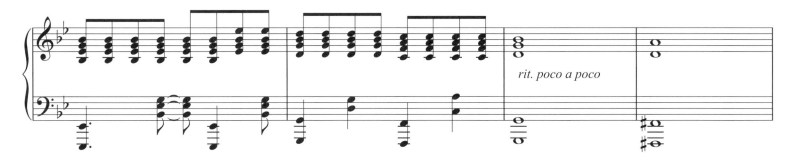

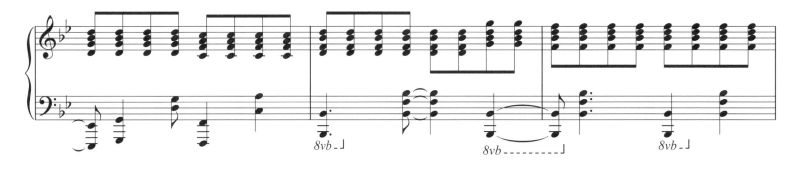

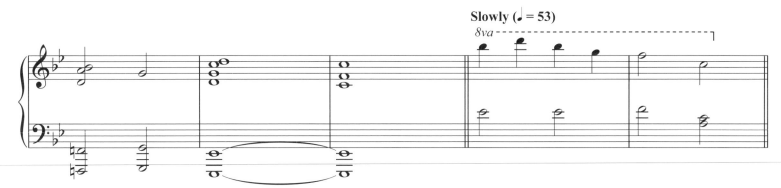

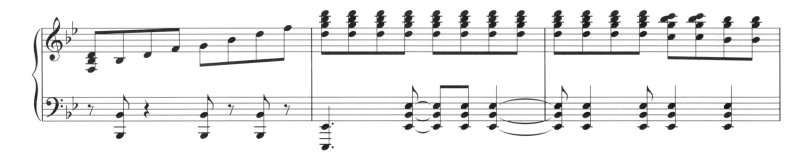

rit.

Slowly (♩ = 52)

Faster (♩ = 138)

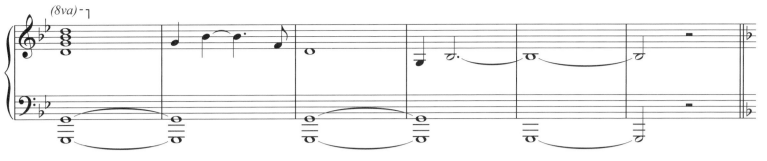

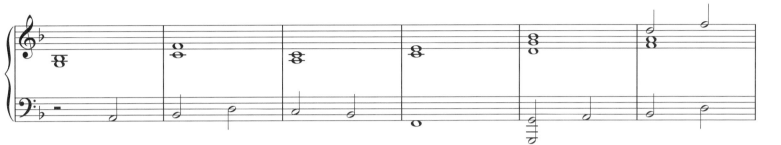

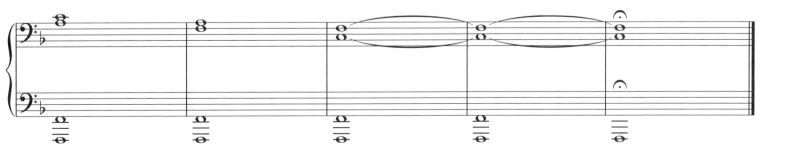

ARIA MATH
from MINECRAFT: VOLUME BETA

By DANIEL ROSENFELD

Andante moderato ($\quarternote$ = 80)

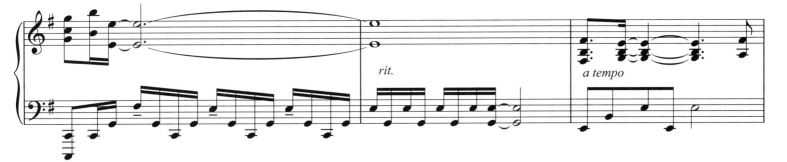

CAT
from MINECRAFT: VOLUME ALPHA

By DANIEL ROSENFELD

Moderately (♩ = 112)

p legato

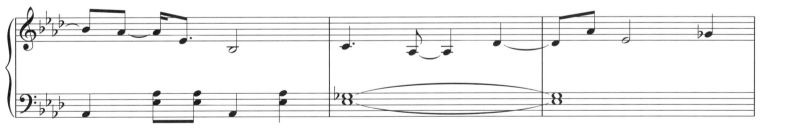

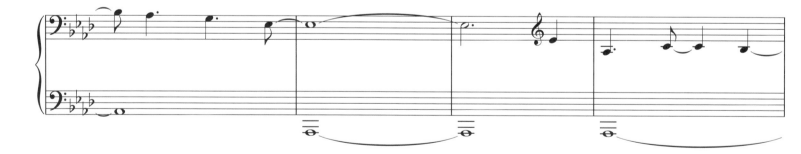

DANNY
from MINECRAFT: VOLUME ALPHA

By DANIEL ROSENFELD

Moderately slow (♩ = 80)

With pedal

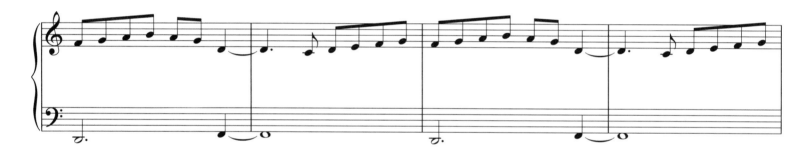

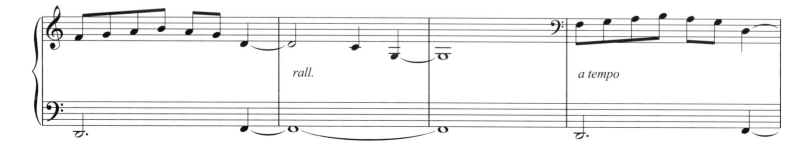

CHIRP
from MINECRAFT: VOLUME BETA

By DANIEL ROSENFELD

Moderately fast (♩ = 110)

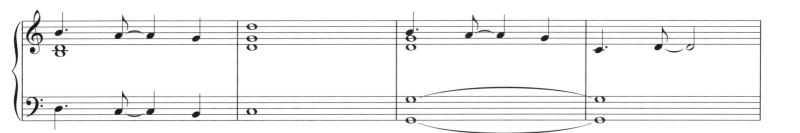

CLARK
from MINECRAFT: VOLUME ALPHA

By DANIEL ROSENFELD

Moderately slow, freely (♩ = 84)

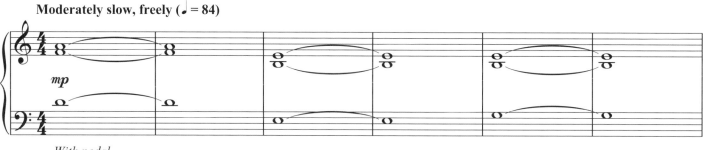

With pedal

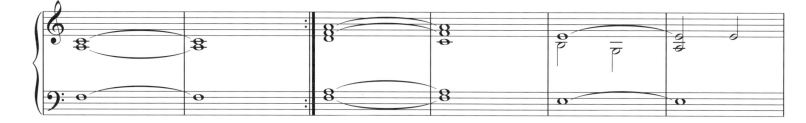

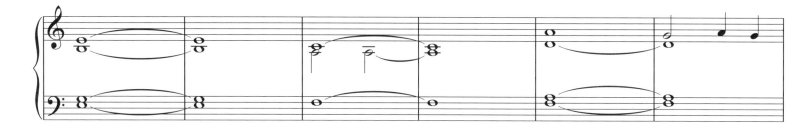

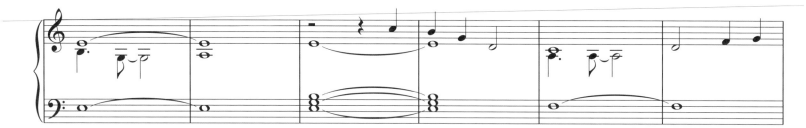

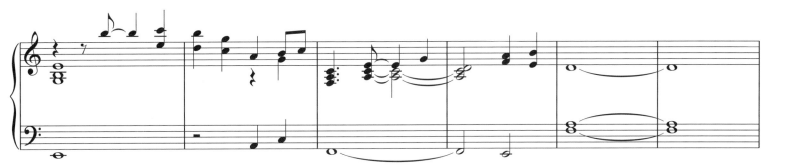

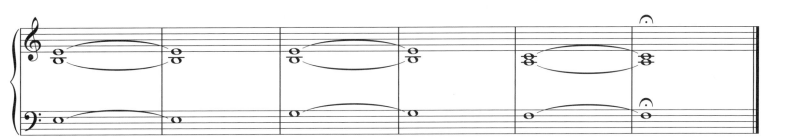

DOOR
from MINECRAFT: VOLUME ALPHA

By DANIEL ROSENFELD

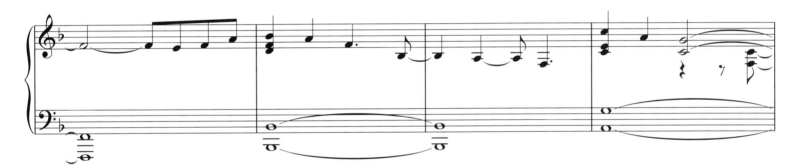

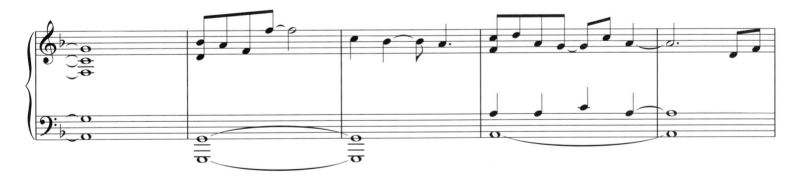

DRY HANDS
from MINECRAFT: VOLUME ALPHA

By DANIEL ROSENFELD

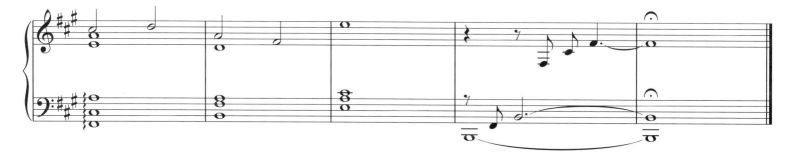

LIVING MICE
from MINECRAFT: VOLUME ALPHA

By DANIEL ROSENFELD

Moderately slow (♩ = 72)

pp

With pedal

cresc.

Repeat and Fade

FAR
from MINECRAFT: VOLUME BETA

By DANIEL ROSENFELD

HAGGSTROM
from MINECRAFT: VOLUME ALPHA

By DANIEL ROSENFELD

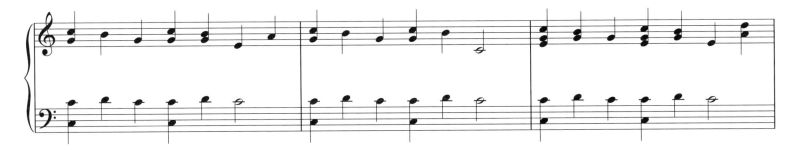

MELLOHI
from MINECRAFT: VOLUME BETA

By DANIEL ROSENFELD

Moderately (♩ = 90)

MICE ON VENUS
from MINECRAFT: VOLUME ALPHA

By DANIEL ROSENFELD

Slowly ($\quarternote$ = 58)

With pedal

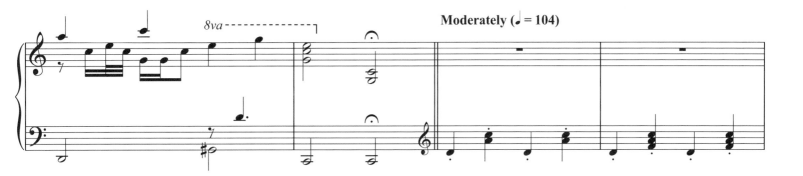

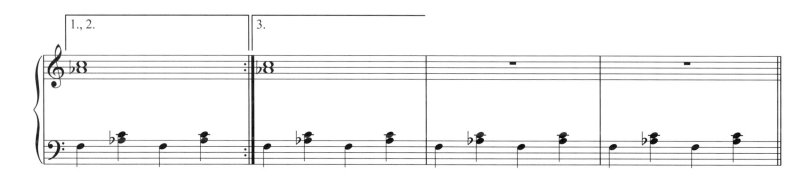

MINECRAFT
from MINECRAFT: VOLUME ALPHA

By DANIEL ROSENFELD

Moderately (♩ = 120)

Repeat ad lib.

Repeat and Fade

MOOG CITY
from MINECRAFT: VOLUME ALPHA

By DANIEL ROSENFELD

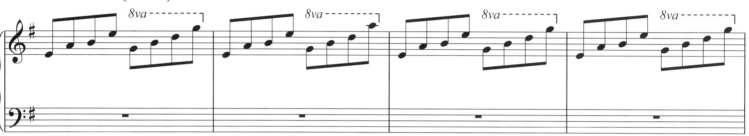

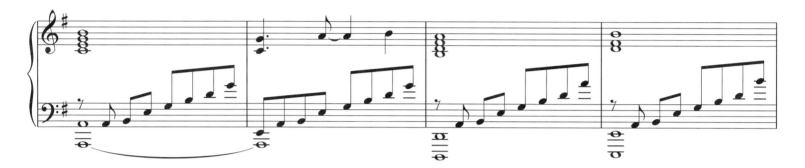

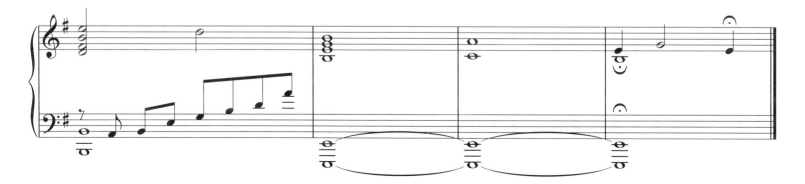

STAL
from MINECRAFT: VOLUME BETA

By DANIEL ROSENFELD

Relaxed Swing (♩ = 105)

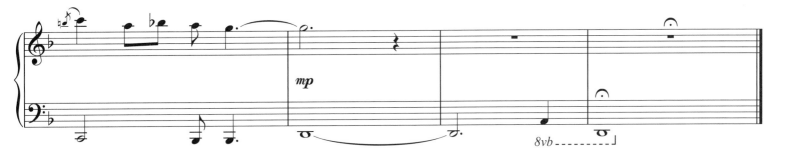

MUTATION
from MINECRAFT: VOLUME BETA

By DANIEL ROSENFELD

Moderately (♩ = 74)

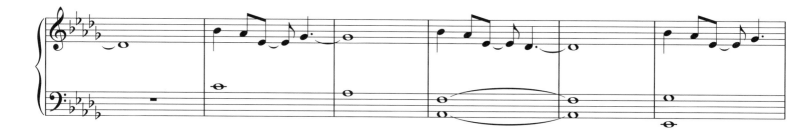

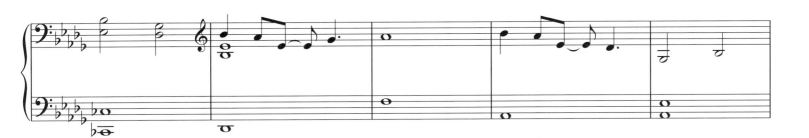

SUBWOOFER LULLABY
from MINECRAFT: VOLUME ALPHA

By DANIEL ROSENFELD

Moderately slow (♩ = 76)

mp

With pedal

Very freely

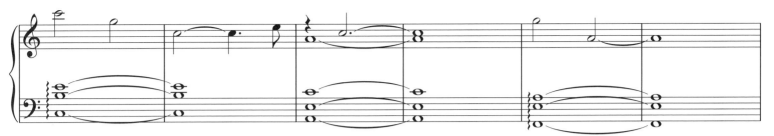

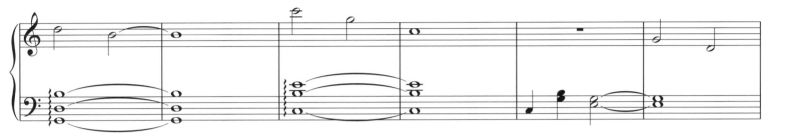

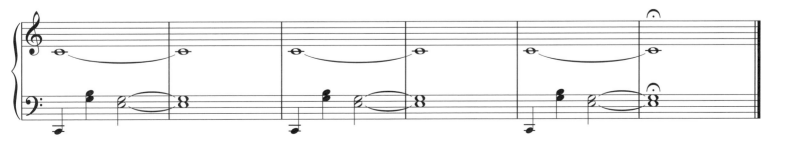

WET HANDS
from MINECRAFT: VOLUME ALPHA

By DANIEL ROSENFELD

SWEDEN
from MINECRAFT: VOLUME ALPHA

By DANIEL ROSENFELD

Slowly

With pedal